A JOURNEY OF LOVE

Lena F. Cole

A JOURNEY
OF LOVE

A Book of
Poems and Inspiration

LENA F. COLE

Published by Omega Publishing Co.

Distributed by Omega Publishing Company.
ISBN 978-0-9986072-0-7
Manufactured in the United States of America

Book Production
LaVerne Harris. of Omega Publishing Company

Dedication

This book is dedicated, first of all, to my Lord and Savior Jesus Christ who blessed me with the gift to write and gave me the mind and heart to live in truth and holiness. I also want to extend this dedication to my children whom I dearly love, Drayla L. Cole,   Daniel J. Cole and my grandchildren LaChristie N. Cole and Blessin L. Thompson.

Acknowledgements

A special thanks to all of my friends and family who have encouraged me over the years. Your support enabled me to reach this goal.

Thank you to my spiritual leaders and Pastor Roosevelt Moore for teaching the uncompromising word of Faith and the spiritual principles shared in this book.

I want to thank my publisher, LaVerne Harris of Omega Publishing Company for all that she did to help make this book a reality. I also give a hearty thanks to you, the reader, for purchasing this book. May it bless your life now and for years to come.

Table of Contents

A LITTLE GIFT TO YOU

To all of my sisters both near and far
You were guided to Jesus by a glistening star.
You are my sisters, both young and old
You are very dear to Jesus' heart, as you have before been told
Listen now my sisters and I will tell you why
I read these words without the least sigh
With joy of love that comes from above
You aren't only my sisters you're mothers too
This is a beautiful gift that comes from the Lord
Where in heaven He sits on the right hand of God
I can imagine Him sending His angels from above
Saying bless this mother and that mother too
Listen carefully my angels as I tell you what to do
These mothers are praying for their children, you hear
I loaned the children to them way over a year
To bring them up from a child and teach them Godly fear
So bless each of these mothers and don't skip not one
I want to congratulate them on a job well done
For they are very dear to Me and My son
Now my dear sisters who are mothers indeed
I'm happy to have you as my sisters in Christ
For surely I speak the truth and no lie
You have many gifts but the greatest is love
That a mother gives to her child who comes from God above
Oh, praise the lord and bless His name forever
For He has made you all mothers, a work that's very clever.

A REASON

There is a reason for everything done or said
A reason for every little turn of the head
Some would think it so simple to be
Having a reason for everything they do, but it is true
I can assure there is a reason for everything to be
A reason for you, a reason for me
There is a reason, I say, for all to be
Look around you, look at the tree, at the sea
There's even a reason for everything you see
God formed the world, He formed the tree
He formed the land and He formed the sea
In his love He formed you and me
Be thankful for the reason God had for forming all things
God's reasons are better than the reasons of man
The reasons of God all his children can withstand
The reasons of man are hard to understand
He'll tell you one reason
and then let another reason stand
There is a reason for everything, I say
And God has made this world full of reasons for His way
I thank God for the reason that He made me.

AN ANNIVERSARY BLESSING

Didn't He let you know that He'd hold you up ?
That he would carry you through
your trials and tribulations too.
All of the times that you were burdened
Didn't He come and see you through?
Look at how He never gave up
Even though He drank from a very bitter cup.
Jesus is not through with you yet.
You'll see when His plan for you completely unfolds,
It will be even more precious
than a beautiful dew dipped rose.
You know, things aren't always what they seem.
Just listen more closely to the voices
of God"s angels as they sing.
You might hear them calling your name
Saying, " Go on be strong!"
"You've come a long way and I'm taking you on."
Don't you know that He loves you so
You're on God's mind all of the time
This is not just a natural anniversary for you.
It is remembered around the throne of God
For all of the things that He's brought you through.
So continue to have a firm hold on God's hand
And He will continue to help you to stand
Beyond all, to stand.
Happy, Happy, Happy Anniversary!

AN ENLARGED HEART

Jesus has an enlarged heart
Big enough for you and me.
Jesus has an enlarged heart
The perfect one has He
His heart has been enlarged
To hold your worries troubles and grief
He came to the earth many years ago
To die upon the cross to set us free.
Jesus has an enlarged heart
to hide your fret and grief.
Do not worry of sickness or pain
It's all been taken away
Jesus has an enlarged heart
God meant it to be that way.
Jesus has an enlarged heart
Big enough for you and me
Jesus has an enlarged heart
The perfect one has He.

ANGELS UNAWARE

When walking down the street on a dreary day
Don't stop walking if a stranger pass your way
Sometimes talking to a stranger is not easy these days
But you never know the stranger
might be an angel unaware
Uplift your eyes to the heavens above
And talk to Jesus who holds you in His love
He will direct you in this day and lead you on
And not let you stray
Hold on to His hand and move at His command
For it is Jesus for whom you'll have to take a stand.
When walking down the street on a long dreary day
don't stop walking if a stranger pass your way.
Sometimes talking to a stranger is not easy these days
But you'd never know, the stranger
might be an angel unaware.
Speak to the stranger, obey God's voice.
Understand what He is saying and move at His command
When He says speak then don't turn your head
For through Jesus' power your mind will be read
Walk on in Jesus name and don't turn around.
Lift up those heads that's been torn down.
For now you are in a city, the city of the living God
And the almighty God's way no man can defraud
Jesus loves you, this is not hard to say
Continue in his love and you will not stray
Don't forget to talk to the stranger
For he might be an angel unaware

BE ASSURED

Don't be pressured into doing things
that you shouldn't do
Look unto Jesus He already
has the way made for you to go through
Hold your head up and walk on in Jesus name
For that's one name that
you'll never be ashamed
Jesus died for us; for you and me
Why can't we be who He wants us to be
Perfect love is what we need
And with that, being in His perfect will
We'll always succeed

I am determined to go on with the Lord .
Hallelujah! I made it through with you Lord
. You are who you are!

BE ENCOURAGED

Jesus holds all things in His hands
He knows the hearts, minds
and even the very thoughts of man
The mighty power of God no man can withstand
There are many things in life that man can't understand
But I know a man named Jesus who can.
When days seem dark and you can't find your way
Fall down on your knees;
put your very thoughts on Jesus
and lift up your voice and pray
Jesus will hear your prayers
He will heed your needs
It's your heart that the eyes of Jesus sees
Jesus loves you, this I can say
For Jesus came to this earth to save souls and not play
His angels are watching
Jesus holds those whom He loves close to His heart
So don't worry and don't you fret
For those whom Jesus loves He never forgets

BELIEVING AND STANDING IN FAITH

People don't seem to care, or see the way I am or want to be. To some, I'm not there simply because the burden is not theirs to bare. I won't fret because I know what's what and I won't dismay because I am in His grace. I have feelings that none seem to care about. To them I am just there.

I know that I am God's child and he cares for me. I have faith in God and I do believe that someday all of my troubles from me He will relieve.

The Lord is so near and dear to me. He won't let me stumble nor make me wander for I'm His child and that's no lie.

The years are coming Yet still going
Stop your mess, stand your test
And let Jesus handle the rest

CALL ON JESUS

When you are walking around
with your head hanging down
Don't let the devil get the best of you
and toss you around
Call on Jesus
The devil will come wearing a crooked toe shoe
He'll throw you a one and
want you to think it's a two
He'll deceive you if you listen but don't
Call on Jesus
Don't sit down and on your face wear a frown
Lift your head up, grasp more faith
and put that devil in a bind
Call on Jesus
If you are in distress
and your soul can't find any rest
Talk to Jesus He knows what is best
Call on Jesus

DISCOURAGED OR DISMAYED

When I've done the best that I can
and my friends don't understand
When I'm walking the lonely pathways
trying hard to reach my goal
And I don't know ; oh, I don't know which way to go
I won't be discouraged, I won't be dismayed
For I know that I will soon
find the road that leads on home
I was walking in the valley through the shadow of death
I was lost as a sinner and was on the wrong road
When I saw a lonely bystander and I asked
"Where is the road that leads on home?"
I won't be discouraged, I won't be dismayed
For I know that I will soon find
the road that leads on home
I pray to the Lord every day to hold my hand
and keep me safe
I need Jesus! Oh I need Jesus everyday
Bless me Lord, Oh most High
Hold my hand by and by
I won't be discouraged I won't be dismayed
Because I know I'll soon find the road that leads on home

DOING GOD'S WILL

When we use our time
to do God's will
He will let us
in His love ever live
Continue to press to make it home
You will surely sit before God
on His heavenly throne
The race was not given to the swift
Nor to the strong
But God gave us His son
to help us make it home .

So much from here to there
Prayer is needed everywhere

DON'T FEAR

The act of being afraid is fear.
Do not be afraid for God is always near.
Fret not of evil doers for God will not fail you.
When times seem hardest is when in
the eyes of Jesus they are most simple.
Be of a sweet mind, be of a sweet spirit,
for the spirit of God is sweet, not being denied.
God is always near, my child, you need not fear.
Just open your mind and talk to Him
as He will always hear.
Don't be dismayed and don't be discouraged
for in Jesus name you can continue to endure.
He is sitting high but He is looking low.
He knows what you are and everywhere you go.
He sends a guiding angel by your side
when down a road of loneliness you have to stride.
He is waiting at the other side, my child,
so just run on and don't get tired.
When you reach the other side,
there will be a light to glisten in your eyes.
Hold your head up and don't get tired.

Remember, Jesus is waiting for you
in His arms for you to abide.
Sometimes things seem hard,
but we should not forget
that it was Jesus who died for us,
the only son that God begat.
He endured the cross that we should not be lost.
Hold His hand and you won't go down.
The act of being afraid is fear.
Be not afraid for God is always near.
God is always near, my friend, you need not fear.
He is sitting high but He is looking low.
He knows what you are and everywhere you go.
Hold your head up and don't get tired.
Don't forget it was Jesus who died for us,
the only son whom God begat.
He endured the cross that we wouldn't be lost.
Hold his hand and you won't go down.

When times come in your life and you don't know what to do. Talk to Jesus He'll instruct you. Bridle your tongue, don't talk too much. That might be the very time when Jesus wants to get in touch.

FACING MY TOMORROWS

I am sitting here tonight writing what I know is right
There is no doubt in my mind
There is no ideas that I have to fight
God has given me a sound mind and I don't feel uptight
There's trials that I go through
There's burdens coming and going too
Yet, I know that it is all in God's hands
He's constantly carrying me through
I'm not afraid of what tomorrow might look like
I face one day at a time
For my Lord and Savior watches over me
As my heart tells me
"My child keep your hands in mine"
Is the words I hear Him speak
So, I will go on
For He has made me strong
For one of my goals
Is to make it to my heavenly home.

FATHER'S DAY

Today is Father's Day
And I wish you the best
Keep your mind on the Lord
Let Him keep you in His rest.
You're God's gift so do the good work
Of a " Jesus name Dad"
Keep Him in your heart and on your mind
Truly Jesus will be with you all of the time.
God made a giftand He formed it well
He left a place for the Holy Ghost to dwell
And for this gift to be called "Dad."
You are God's great wonder
Being called and dedicated for His plan.
Walk in holiness before Him
And He will keep you
in the palm of His hands.

FOR YOUR LOVE

For your love
I wish I could climb the highest mountain
I wish I could swim the deepest sea
For your love
I would do these things
If it meant being together
for you and me
For your love
I would write the sweetest poem
I would sing the sweetest song
Paper could not hold
the things I would do
Just for your love
For you and me to come true

Jesus is my help
I will make it with the Lord
As my guide

FORGIVENESS

No matter what the situation is
We must forgive our bretheren
and do God's will
It's not hard to forgive
if the heart is right
So why should one walk around
feeling so uptight?
As God forgave us for our horrible sin
So are we to forgive our fellow men
And God is a spirit;
He is truth
If we don't forgive each other as He says
Then He won't carry us through
So come on people
and let's do it right
Forgive me if I have offended you
and I'll forgive you to.

FRIENDS AND FAMILIES

A friend is someone whom God
Has given you to be close in heart to.
Someone who will be there at all times
No matter what you go through.
Remember there is a friend
Who sticks closer than a brother. Jesus!
Families---God has given us both spiritual and natural.
With God as the head it will be everlasting.
We can all be friends in Christ
And families in the Lord
As long as we live our lives for Him
And let Him in our hearts.

I don't want no "hip Hop.
I don't want no "rock n roll"
I only want Jesus name
Something that will save my soul

GET ON YOUR WAY UP

I'm on my way up and I ain't turning around
Jesus has a hold and I can't come down
He has washed my soul and set me free
He won't let the devil upset me
If you wanna get right don't give the devil time
Cause he'll step right in and mess up your mind
Just get on your way up
And don't turn around
Let Jesus get a hold and you won't come down
If you turn to Satan once, He'll try to get you twice
He'll talk to you so you want even try
So get on your way up and make up your mind
Give God a chance , he's right on time
If you wanna get right then turn from envy and strife
God will talk to you, he knows the way of your heart
Just get on your way up and get in God's line
Serve the Lord with a holy mind
Just get on your way up and don't turn around
Let Jesus get a hold and you won't come down

GOD HAS POWER

The thunder roars, the lightning flash
The rain falls and the streets flood
God makes this to happen
He has power over heaven and earth
God has power over the whole universe

We come to the light and repent of our sin
We get baptized in Jesus name
and go on and live holy for Him
God makes this to happen
He has power over the wind
He has power over the rain
He has power over you
and He has power over me the same

When you are in a trial and your head is hung down
He sends His angel to lift your head up
And over your face He puts a smile

He removes the frown
that caused your head to hang down
He gives us more courage
and strength to go many more miles

God has power over the fowl of the air
He has power over the fish of the sea
He has power over the beast of the field
And don't forget, just remember
God has power over you and me

Jesus is here I can tell after going through trials. Still all seems well and I put my trust in the Lord. Even though I don't bet, for I know the truth. He's still holding my hand and walking with me yet.

GOD IS IN CONTROL

God is in control of the wind
He is in control of the sea, he is in control of you
and all that around you be.
If god calmed the raging storm,
healed the sick and raised the dead
What more will he do if we by his spirit are led.
God is in control
Don't be discouraged and don't be dismayed
If it seems that all things around you are in disarray.
Hold your head up and walk in faith,
For Jesus will fix it for you just like
He did in the bible days.
God is in control
Believe with your heart, believe with your soul
Cast all of your cares upon the Lord and let Him your
burdens hold.
Don't be discouraged and don't be dismayed,
Believe that Jesus is holding your hand
and that it is He who will help you to stand
Just remember that
God is in control

GODS POWER

I don't wait until times seem hard
To fall on my knees
and let Jesus make intersession for me to God
I don't wait until a burden befalls me
To fall down and cry at Jesus' feet
I shout and praise His name
I cry tears of joy when all is going well
I cry tears of sadness when one of God's children,
hurt has befallen.
Jesus is waiting to answer our calls
When on His everlasting name we do call
He'll lift up the hearts that have fallen down
He'll refresh the joy that needs to be found
I'll walk on in Him
For He is my strength
In Him I know my soul He will from evil prevent.

HE IS THE WAY

The Lord leadeth me in the path of His righteousness
I shall not fear what men shall do or say
For God has put me in a sacred place to stay.
I was alone and didn't know what to do.
I fell on my knees to talk to Jesus
And surely He has brought me through.
Listen to me people and listen to me good.
You can't live in this life without Jesus Christ.
For without him it is just jealousy, envy,
wrath, heresies and strife.
Serve the Lord with a pure and sincere heart
And from your life He'll never depart.
Trust in the Lord for He is good
And to Jesus Christ you are understood.

"HE'S A- LISTENING TO MY CALL"

He won't forsake me , He knows all about me
He has made a way for me that only He and I can see
"King Jesus is a listening to my call"
I sit on my bed and drop my head
But I know that soon I'll be heavenly lead
I wonder if the rest of the world's in a horrible twirl
or standing on a bend
barely slipping through thick and thin
Looking for their only friend, but I know
"King Jesus is a listening to my call"
I love the Lord and He hears my plea
And lends His eyes when I can't see
He's very loving, kind and true
If only we could be the same way too
I'm not afraid to lift my head for I know I'll be led
I love the lord and He is so good
He does things I never could
I will not fret or never regret For things will get better
and still better yet I love the Lord and always will
He hears my plea and answers me still
"King Jesus is a listening to my call"

HE'LL BE RIGHT THERE

When you are walking down a long lonely road
That seems to be leading nowhere
When it seems that you have no friends
Or it seems that no one cares
Just reach your heart out to Jesus
He'll be right there
When times seem to get a little hard
When it seems you can't go on
Even though you made a start
You don't know what to do
But you need someone to help you go through
Just reach your heart out to Jesus
He'll be right there
When you don't know which way to go
Sometimes situations arise
That makes you wanna turn around and run
You try to remember the point
from which you first begun
Run on to Jesus he'll engulf you in His arms
Just reach your heart out to Jesus
He'll be right there

HUMBLE UNTO THEE

I was sitting at my table one cold and dreary day
My children were running and skipping
For they were at play
As I looked at my children, it seemed I heard a voice say
"Humble they are, this is my will for all, you see.
As humble as a child in my eyes to be."
I knew at once that this was the Lord speaking to me.
For I had prayed, "Lord make me humble,
More humble unto Thee"
God answers our prayers in ways that we don't expect.
When we ask him things, He doesn't forget.
He comes in His own time to show us what's best.
I'll never forget that dreary day
That turned beautiful as I listened
to what the Lord had to say.

I HEARD SOMEBODY CALLING MY NAME

I was living in a world of sin
I did not know my enemies from my friends
I was going over here and doing all of that
People said "child do this and child do that."
Down in my heart I was hurting so bad
I didn't have no place for my soul to be fed
I needed the Lord down in my soul
I needed the Lord to come take control
I cried "Lord Lord come see about me.
Outstretch your hands and have mercy please."
He stretched out His hands in the world of sin
He reached right down and pulled me in
He said, "My child, I love you, can't you see
I heard your cry and I answered your plea.
Now serve me child every day that you live,
And in My holy mountain be still."
I heard somebody calling my name
I heard somebody calling my name
I heard somebody calling my name
I looked around and Jesus came

I KNOW WHO THE DEVIL IS!

It's the devil''s business to make things
seem like what they aren't
To fight you against those who love you so much
If you're just wandering with your head hung down
Hold your head up before the devil
be camping on your ground
When you give in to the devil he just laughs,
he means you no good
He just wants you to be his everlasting fool
The devil is hanging around in this town
He's pacing the streets up and down
He's just waiting to park one of his spirits at your place
So stay prayed up, stay encouraged and don't dismay
When the devil knocks at your door
He won't be able to lead you astray
It's good to know who the devil is when he comes around
For he sure drops his unclean spirits all over town
Rebuke them, resist them and don't play around
For the devil has no power
over a Jesus name child

I KNOW WHO'S HOLDING MY HAND

Maybe I can't walk 50 miles or jump 50 leaps
Maybe I can't climb the highest mountain
or a hill that's too steep
But I know who's holding my hand
and my soul He's gonna keep
I am the captain of my ship
God is the keeper of my soul
He has promised me eternal life,
put my name on His holy roll
My heavenly father watches over me
He has planted me as a tree,
well set and preserved for thee
Maybe I can't walk 50 miles or jump 50 leaps
Maybe I can't climb the highest mountain
or a hill that's too steep
But I do know who's holding my hand
And my soul He's gonna keep

I SAID A PRAYER FOR YOU

I said a prayer for you last night
I felt that everything would be alright
When you stand up for the Lord and do what He says
There is no mistake about it
God already has your way paved.
So keep walking on and obey His voice
Even when things seem to get hard
Hear the still small voice saying
"Be still, I said a prayer for you last night"

I will stand up straight and stay this race
For I know that God has me
steadfast in His grace
I wanna please God and not man
What's so hard about that,
You don't understand.

I WILL STAND IN HIS POWER

The devil is a lie and he won't get by
He can't cause division between God's people
So there's no reason for him to try.
I will hold my head up and walk on in faith
For one day I know I'm gonna reach that heavenly place
Where I will sit down at Jesus' feet
And my eyes, His will meet.
For He has given me the power over the devil to defeat
God holds my life in His hands
I know that in Jesus I have made a " Jesus name" stand
I will continue to stand, I will stand and stand
For I know that Jesus is truly holding my hand
When times seem hard, Jesus is always near
He makes me stronger
when the devil tries to make me fear.
I will run on, I will not fall
For Jesus has raised me up to serve him
For He is my all in all
I will continue to be glad and rejoice in Him
For He has saved my soul and has made me whole

IN HIS WILL

Cry no more, wipe your tears
The Holy Ghost has come to comfort your fears
Rejoice in the Lord, this is His people's heart intent
When you turn the devil aside
Jesus will take away all sinful pride

You have a race to run but it can't be run in stride
Be sure not to turn to the devils side
Jesus has a table where you can be fed
He has plenty of heavenly bread
Just open your ears and eat with a pure heart
Take heed to this bread
and your life won't from Jesus depart

Jesus has plans for the pure in heart, you see
But you gotta have the Holy Ghost for these plans to be
Love the Lord with all of your heart
Continue on with Him
For now you have made a heavenly start

IN REMEMBRANCE

Thinking of the days that you were among us
How you sang sweet songs
And Jesus' spirit was there as a witness
In remembrance
Thinking of how you danced before the Lord and
How His Glory shown on and around you
How you laughed and showed much love
In remembrance
Thinking of how you would tease,
And how I would meddle when you played the piano
How you would pick at me playing the tambourine
In remembrance
Just thinking of the good times we had in the Lord
But believing God that soon all over again they will start
His angels are watching, He holds these things in regard
You're missed and you're loved so very much
You'll be back, I do not fret
For the prayers of the righteous, Jesus never forgets

INSIDE THIS VESSEL

I am just a vessel put together by the strong hands of my master. Inside of the vessel, there lies no empty shallow hole like in a tin vessel. Inside this vessel there is breath. Inside this vessel there is sight. Inside this vessel there is touch. Inside this vessel there is smell. Inside this vessel, there is love. Inside this vessel there is hope. Inside this vessel there is belief. Inside this vessel, there is faith. Inside this vessel, all of these things dwell, put here by the mighty hands of my master.

There is no shallowness inside this vessel. There is no hate inside this vessel; no envy or strife. My master is not the author of these things, so inside this vessel, he did not put them. There are other vessels also. You are one. Do you know what's inside your vessel?

Let Jesus make you a vessel of His perfect will and then you'll know that you are not a vessel of any ungodly ill. Think on this. Is your vessel clean? Let Jesus use it for His means.

I'VE BEEN CHANGED

There was a time in my life
When I had nothing but pain, trouble and strife
My life was a mess I must confess
I needed peace and I needed rest
I wanted the Lord to help my soul
But I was so bound up
that I couldn't let Him take complete control
I went to one place to try and be saved
But I soon realized
I was getting closer to the grave
You see, I was taught that I could do anything
Which meant that I wouldn't be
on God's holy team
But, oh one day, I fell to my knees
And God's true power flowed through me
Since that day I
haven't been the same
For truly I've heard
Jesus calling my name.

INSPIRATION

Sitting here waiting for the inspiration to come
waiting for the inspiration to write a poem
I thought I'd fondle with my words a while
Maybe I'd come up with some cute little word
to put upon someone's face a pretty smile
I'll mix my words and come up with a rhyme
I want to make it sweet
but not to be sold even for a dime
I am writing it from the bottom of my heart
for it was Jesus who gave me the writing start.
While sitting here waiting for the inspiration to come,
I think that I've almost written a poem.
Don't laugh too hard if at first you begin to giggle,
for while I was writing it I got a little tickled.
I am satisfied now for I have written a poem
and no longer do I have to wait
for the inspiration to come.

JESUS AND ME

Sitting here, my head is not down
Nor am I on my face wearing a frown
I came to Jesus while my life was turned around
He helped me overcome the world and gave me power
So that the devil can't turn my life upside down
I am living this life for Jesus,
My friend you see
He called me into His Holy Ghost rest
And my whole life from that day on has been blessed.
So get back devil, wherever you are
For I am going on with Jesus
For I have come this far

Get back devil, you can't win
You can't come around
and cause me to sin
You stupid devil, I hate you so
You are already on the list
for "death row"

JESUS CARES

It's not as hard as it might seem
Sometimes the devil wants you to feel
as if you are hanging out on a string
But be patient , run on and be content
For in your life
God is gonna let come
exactly what is meant
So when times seem hard
and you don't know what to do
Look up to Jesus dear
He'll carry you through
Jesus will not let come
no more than you can bear
Jesus died on the cross
to show you that he cares
Dear, when you are tried and its time for the test
Don't give up your faith
for Jesus has you in His Holy Ghost rest
And remember child, Jesus cares

JESUS HAS THE ANSWERS

There are a lot of things that's been left unsaid
There are a lot of things that's been left unread
But in this life I've found it best
To handle my business and let God take care of the rest
Jesus has the answers
I'll continue to read the bible and take heed to what it says
For it is the word of God that's gonna keep me
walking in God's holy ghost ways
Jesus has the answers
Today I can say I have made it through another year
Jesus has blessed me to live for him
I will not fear what the devil has to say
For I know it is Jesus
Who is keeping my soul and
has kept it up until this very day.
Jesus has the answers
Jesus is near, he is ever so dear
Jesus has the answers
He has the answers, you hear!

JESUS IS HOLDING YOUR HAND

While walking in Jesus' way,
don't let the devil lead you astray
He'll do all he can to interfere with Gods'plan,
but remember
Jesus is holding your hand
The devil is going to and fro
seeking whom he may destroy
As he knocks on your door, don't let your hedge down
He'll know there's no reason for him
to knock or hang around
Jesus is holding your hand
It is no sin to be tempted by the devil
Just don't give in
Then by this no sin can be found
He's the author of sin and sin is the cause of death
But you have the devil beat
On your soul he cannot bring forth wrath
Walk on in Jesus and be content
To the devil give no consent
Just remember, Jesus is holding your hand

JESUS, MY SAVIOR

You don't have to worry and you don't have to fret
For Jesus is watching over you, don't you forget.
The Lord has a reason for everything he does.
His reasons are not reasons for human eyes to see.
Just keep your mind stayed on God
He wants you in His grace where you will never depart.
Look up to Jesus for he is always near
Even when things happen in your life
that wants to cause you fear
JESUS WILL
Catch a hold of Jesus' guiding hand
Don't break down when something takes place
that you don't understand
Remember that Jesus is near
and he knows what's going on.
For it is in Jesus name that you're gonna be made strong
Hold on to Jesus and don't let him go.
For everyday he loves you more, more and even more
Remember there is a reason for everything that God does
And His reasons are not reasons for the human eye to see.

JESUS WILL

In Jesus grace he'll hold you still,
He will protect you, my friend, from all ungodly ill.
He'll hold your hand and won't let you fall.
Just cast all of your trust upon him.
Cling to him and when times seem hard
He'll help you to stand.
Hold on, my friend, don't be afraid.
Call out to Jesus, he'll hear your plea.
He'll come see about you
I know because he did the same thing for me
JESUS WILL

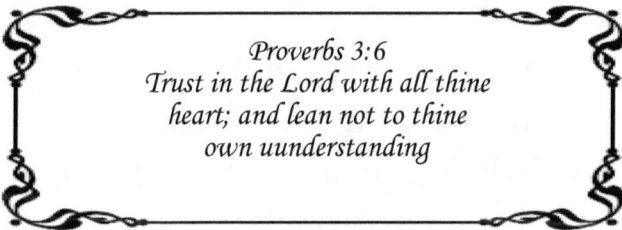

Proverbs 3:6
Trust in the Lord with all thine
heart; and lean not to thine
own uunderstanding

JESUS WILL

Don't ever tell Jesus what you can't do
For if it's his will he'll surely see you through
Jesus will

Just ask Him for strength to help you go through
Put all of your trust in him He'll tell you what to do
Jesus will

He'll help you pass your trial's
He'll ease your tribulations too
Seek Him for an answer He'll take care of you
Jesus will

He's taking care of me, He'll do it for you
Trust in Jesus, He never fails
Live for Jesus, He'll give you a great testimony to tell
Jesus will

JESUS WILL GUIDE YOU

Things might not seem to be looking up
But just keep your eyes on Jesus
for He is gonna fill your cup
When it seems that you have come to your roads end
It is usually when Jesus steps in
and your life really begins
So don't be discouraged and don't be dismayed
Jesus has already opened the door
and your way has been paved.
Jesus has beautiful things in store for you
When you do what He tells you to do.
So pray on, hold your head up
and don't be in doubt
For its Jesus my friend who has promised
and will bring you out
He will, I say, He will indeed
He'll bring you out,
Just hold fast and you'll see.

JESUS WILL NEVER FORGET

You don't ever have to worry;
you don't ever have to fret
Because your soul Jesus will never forget
He is sitting high but is looking down low
He'll forever hold your hand If you don't let go
He created the sun. He created the Moon
He created the garden and the flowers to bloom
He created you. He created me
He created our hands to touch and our eyes to see
Keep Him in your heart
Keep Him in your mind
He'll soon make a way for your light to shine
Just cling to the Lord with all your heart
And from the Lord you'll never depart
You don't ever have to worry;
you don't ever have to fret
Because His children Jesus never forgets

LOOK

Look at the view of the beautiful things
That God made for you and for me.
He made the sun to shine, the flowers to bloom
He made the rain to fall and the birds to sing
He made the grass to grow and the trees to bud
He made the animals to be
and He made the fish to swim
Look at the beautiful things that God has done
He gave His only begotten son
He let him be hung upon a tree
He let him die for you and me
He never said not one word
When " crucify him". " crucify him"
was the words that He heard
We should be glad and rejoice in Him
For when He died, He had committed no sin
We should be glad and rejoice in Him
Now we have a great reason to want to make it in
Of all of the things that God has done
One of the most beautiful things is when
He gave His only begotten son.

LOOK AROUND YOU

People look around you and see what you can see.
Is there a bird sitting in a tree?
Is there a flower being stung by a bee?
Is there a dog that's being bit by a flea?
Is there a cloud in the sky or did someone just die?
People look around you and see what you can see.
I know that God made this world
the way that He wants it to be.
Why do you fear or why do you fret
When your way you can't always get?
Don't be afraid and don't be ashamed
When someone walks up and asks you
if you believe in Jesus' name
God has a plan for your life you see.
That is if His will you will let be.
Open your eyes for it was Jesus who died.
It was His body that He offered up for a sacrifice.
Run on in Him and don't turn around
For Jesus will never let you down.
People look around you and see what you can see.
God has made a way for you and me.
But He gave His only and own son to die on the tree.
He let His son offer up His own body for a sacrifice for you and me.
Never forget what God has done.
Remember, He gave His only begotten son.

LORD HELP HIM

Lord help him to be what you want him to be
Let him understand that he is a tree
that you want to be planted unto thee
Keep him safe, guide him
where you want him to go
From the door of disgust
turn him to a better light
Keep him Lord and use him to be your knight
Lord help him to think on
what you want him to do
Lord you see, he is so nice, kind and true
I know Lord that this kind
can be used by you
Strengthen him Lord, in your right
Comfort his heart
and help him to do what's right
See to it, Lord, that he does your will
So that when he hears your voice
He'll know that it was you who kept him still
Lord help him

LOVE

Love is like the waters
as they are calmed in the sea
Not tossing to and fro
as the raging waters would be
Love is like the sound
of the birds singing in the trees
As though sending out a message
to put a heart at ease
Love is in the world needing to find its place
If we open up our hearts and minds to it
Love will find its way
Love is a beautiful thing
To have in our heart
Love is what it's gonna take
To give us a new start

MY BATTLE

The world is harsh, my friends are few
but I have Jesus with me
I know I'll make it through
I made up my mind not to live of the world
The devil is mad but I am glad
Cause he don't have any power over me
He keeps trying, poor thing
But he just can't see
I've been made strong
in the power of God's might
I rise to the challenge
when it is time to fight
The devil is defeated
each and every day
Because God's word tell me
Just what I need to say

MY BIRTHDAY

Now the old year has gone
And a new year has come along
I prayed to the Lord,
please move this year
And let things of the past be bygone
God sees the heart
And He's the one who makes it strong
You please the Lord and I'll please Him too
Then we won't have time to say
What others ought to do
I'm holding on to God's unchanging hand
For I plan to see His glorious promised land

Proverbs 14:33a
Wisdom resteth in the heart of him
that hath understanding;

MY GIFT

God gave me this gift I can't resist. I must continue to write no matter how hard the devil fights. You see when God gives you something to do, you must do it with all your might. Yes, with all your might because Jesus has given you that right.

No matter how things might seem or look in the eyes of man. Know that in Jesus you can conquer all things, yes you can.

We're going up higher to another level you see. Jesus will be there to meet us and the climb is not too steep. He's teaching us how things must be done in His name. We've got to leave the old behind, press on and continue to climb.

Don't watch me and I won't watch you. Let's keep our eyes on the Lord as He tells us what to do.

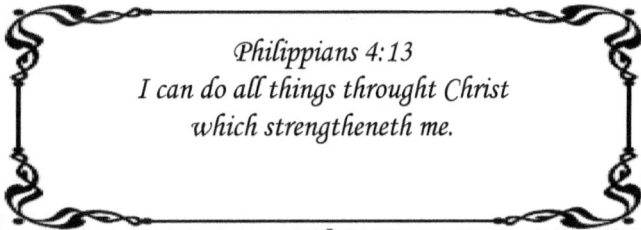

Philippians 4:13
I can do all things through Christ
which strengtheneth me.

MY HEAVENLY HOME

I am determined to run on until the end
I am determined that to the old devil,
I won't give in
Jesus has done many sweet things for me
It was Jesus who set me free
I will run on and not get tired
Because on the cross for me
Jesus gave up His life
I'll stick with Him, I won't be afraid
For I know Jesus is standing
in His father's stead
I'll just run this race unto the end
For I have Jesus as an everlasting friend
I am pressing to reach my heavenly home
Where I will see God sitting on
His heavenly throne
I know He's waiting to welcome me in
For He has made me free from sin

NOT MY OWN

My life is not mine,
it's in God's command
He has a reason for the sand to flow
and the oars to row
My house is built not on sand,
but on the solid rock it's gonna stand
The obstacles put in my life
is not paid for by the devil's fare
But for God to keep me in constant prayer
My soul is his, other things He will heal
I look not to the left nor to the right
for the battle is Jesus,
in His name, helps me to fight
The devil has no room,
I have not to presume
My life is not my own,
but to Sarah I was born
God's angel is leading
and I'm constantly believing
that in Jesus hand I'll keep my stand.

OF INSPIRATION

Fight the devil and hold out until the end
Let that devil know that to his side you won't give in
He has lost many battles he's tried to take over
And this is another battle where he will lose control
The devil don't want you to hold to the Lord's hand
Cause he knows that Jesus will help you to stand

The race is not given to the swift nor the strong
But it is given to those who hold on
Hold on with all that you have in your soul
And don't let the devil interfere with your goal
We are tried in different ways
But God awards those
Who from his ways never stray

Remember God rules the holy ghost rest
After we do what we can
He takes over and finishes the rest
When all hope seems gone God's power will prevail
Hold to his hand for He never fails

We're not tempted above what we are able to stand
So hold on stand, stand and just stand
You know we prosper by the things that we suffer
But Jesus makes us strong so that
fighting old Satan we are much tougher

God makes us into what he wants us to be
His reasons we cannot always see
But He holds out His hands to welcome us in
He is our one and dearest true friend
So run on in Jesus and don't give up
For Jesus, my friend, loves you very much

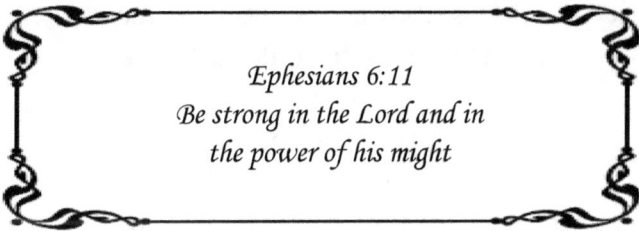

Ephesians 6:11
Be strong in the Lord and in
the power of his might

ONCE

Once I was alone and living in distress
I had no peace of mind, my soul had no rest
I heard of the man Jesus
To whom my sins I did confess

Once I did not know which way to go
For all of the places I had gone
I didn't want to go any more

Once I didn't know just what to do
I talked to so many people
But they couldn't help me see my way through

Jesus sent his angel down from His throne
He commanded him to come and teach me
The right way to make it home

Now of a surety my soul is at peace
For it is the word of God
On which my soul likes to feast

PLEASE, DON'T GO TO HELL!

Please don't go to hell
the fire is much too hot
Down there is no place
where you can praise God or shout
Please don't go to hell the
fire is much too hot
For when the flames start to blaze,
In your mind will be no doubt
Please don't go to hell
the fire is much too hot
Down there is no cure
for the burning foot shock
Please don't go to hell
the fire is much too hot
Down there is no mountains to climb
Or stumbling blocks to walk around
For you would have already
stumbled your last time
You'll be burning for the rest of eternity
Please don't go to hell
the fire is much too hot

POEM TO MY GRANDDAUGHTER

God has blessed you with this
Your special day again
He has given you a beautiful smile
And a beautiful grin.
He loves and cares for you a lot
I love you too, you know my dear
But it was God and his son Jesus
who brought you here.
He has a special angel with you too
You can't see him
but he's watching over you
Grow up, be happy and always remember
To thank God for giving
you this and every day.
Happy Birthday, Sweeten.
Happy Birthday to you.
I love you little one
and this is so true.
Happy Birthday, Sweeten.
Happy Birthday to you !

PRAISE GOD

Praise God! Praise God!
Praise him for all His mighty acts
Praise God from whom all your blessings flow
Praise Him for not letting you
go back into the world anymore
Praise God for truly He has brought you out,
Out of the sinful world without a doubt.
Praise God for His mighty acts,
Praise Him for where He now have you at
Praise Him in the morning,
Praise Him in the noon,
praise Him in the night
For you can never praise Him too soon
Don't be afraid to call upon His name
Clap your hands, stomp your feet, rejoice in Him
For you know your prayers He did meet.
Look upon the Lord with all of your might
Hold your head up
Continue to walk upright
Rejoice in the Lord for He is so good
He brought you out of the world
where the devil never could

Be of sound mind,
be of good cheer
For remember my friends,
Jesus is always standing near
He knows your heart
and the thoughts of your mind
He heeds your plea
He is always right on time
Go on and obey God
in whatsoever he tells you to do
And when your trials
and tribulations come,
He'll be right there
to carry you through.
Remember the Lord for He is so good
He has done things for us
that the carnal man never could
Don't forget the Lord is near
He hears your prayers
and He loves you dear.

RUN MY CHILD

Run, run, take shelter quick
Flee, flee, get away from here
In this town you cannot stay
Danger is coming, it's on its way

You must strive to stay alive
You must fight to survive
Make haste people, do not tarry
Danger is coming, and it's on its way

I can imagine hearing these words
As they rang through the town
Before it was turned upside down

Psalm 91:4
He will cover thee with His pinions and
under his wings shalt thou take refuge

SATAN HAS LOST HIS GROUND

Sometimes the devil comes in strong
His wish is for us to lose our ground.
But that old devil isn't quite enough wise
So he can just get off the battle ground.
He'll throw a rock of offense
in God's people's way
But for a surety, God's people will not go astray.
He's just wasting his time
wanting God's people to be torn down
He doesn't have a stand,
he has already lost his ground.
He'll take a one and try to make it look like two
He'll try to show his horns
and tell you what to do
Not obeying what he tells you to do,
He'll leave and come again
wearing another crooked shoe
He dosen't have a stand,
he has already lost his ground.

SING A SONG

Sing a song to Jesus
Sing it with all your might
Open up your heart and let the sunshine in
Jesus wantS you to make melody in your heart
Who knows this might be the way
That Jesus will give you a brand new start
Jesus died for you, and he died on the cross
He hung there and died
so that your soul wouldn't be lost.
Sing a song to Jesus. Sing with all of your might
Open up your heart and let the sunshine in
My friend why don't you sing a song tonight?
God gave you His son, He had only one
But He gave you His son
Why can't you sing Him a song?
He loves your soul, let Him take control
Let Him come in to make you free from sin
Be truthful in your heart
Open up and let the light shine in.
Sing a song to Jesus
Sing it with all of your might
Open up your heart and let the sunshine in
My friend , why don't you sing a song tonight?

SPREAD YOUR ARMS ALL OVER ME

Come on be my mother, come on be my father
Spread your arms all over me
Come on be my sister, come on be my brother
Spread your arms all over me

Lord talk to me, Lord hold my hand
Let me know that you understand
Come on Lord
Spread your arms all over me

When I was down in sin, you spoke within
You let me know that you were real
You opened the door and took me in
Spread your arms all over me

I love you Lord and I won't go astray
I'm in this holy word to stay
Come on Lord
Spread your arms all over me

Spread your arms all over me, spread your arms
All over me. This life is real, I know it is,
This holy life keeps me still. Come on Lord,
Spread your arms all over me.

STANDING TOGETHER

Let us not be discouraged
When we are doing well
Keep your mind on Jesus
And you will have a testimony to tell.

We're fighting a war
Against the wiles of the devil
We mustn't let him
Bring us down to his level

Let us be on one mind
And on one accord
Let us be in unity
With the spirit of Jesus Christ our Lord

We're still precious jewels
Chosen and sought out by the Lord
So let's keep Him in our hearts
As our maker to regard

Let's not be discouraged
Let's keep our hearts lifted up
Looking unto Jesus
And drinking from His sweet flowing cup

TAKE HEED MY CHILD

Can't you see that the Lord is after you
And that is why things are not going
the way that you want them to.
Move on up and do what the Lord requires
And you'll see how things
will improve in your life.
Jesus is waiting for your knock on the door
There are many things he'd like for you to know
He wants you to give your whole life to Him
Put it in His hands and let Him take control .
You are His, you know. You are His very own
He is the author of your life
and He is the keeper of your soul
Jesus is knocking at your heart.
Can't you feel the tapping?
He's pulling at your heartstrings;
Can't you feel the tug?
Don't ignore him. Open up and let Him in
For it is with Jesus only
that you are gonna win.

THE COMPASS POINT

I am not as strong as I would like to be. I am only a common human being who has no more powers than those seen fit by my master. I cannot control the passing of time or its endeavors.

A compass point has no definite stop or start. Who can control one of such motive . Time is the symbol of this compass point. The battle of the ships stand steadfast upon its recovery grounds, I wish not to interfere.

I have a motive that is too complicated for the immoral man to understand. Hope, whether it appears to be or not, is one of the basic struggles of the compass which has no point.

But I am the captain of my ship and God is the keeper of my soul. With these words my faith and belief will behold the oncoming and steadiness of the passing of times indefinite compass point. It has only one ideal motivation and that is " to pass on by."

THE HOUSE ON
THE HILL

I stood there and looked at the house on the hill
The windows were all closed, the shutters were all sealed
The paint was worn, the roof caving in
"Oh my god", I thought
what a beautiful house this must have been
I began to shake as my body caught a chill
For I thought of my savior hanging on Golgatha's hill
Even though I knew it was a prophecy fulfilled
Wondering how he would feel
at the sight of this house on the hill
This house needed repair, a great many to be done
For no one could see the beauty of it
For it was all weather beaten and worn
"If only…", I thought, "if someone would fix it up
Turn it into a beautiful house,, put it to some use
Not let it waste any longer, build it up and make it stronger"
I started to feel better as a gentle touch in my heart I felt
I heard a voice say "My child it will be fixed,
it will be well kept.
I have a plan for this house, you see.
It's gonna be a vessel of honor set and well kept by me."
Right then I knew without a doubt
It was Jesus who was gonna work this out
I can't explain the feeling I felt as I stood there at that moment
But I know t I will never feel there is no hope for a house
Torn, weather beaten or worn
Whether sitting on a hill or sliding down a slope
When Jesus loves you there is always hope

THE LORD IS GOOD

The Lord has been mighty good to me
A whole new year
He has allowed me to see
He held on to my hand
When I felt like I couldn't go on
He gave me more strength
and made me strong
The Lord is so precious to me
He opened doors for me
that I couldn't see
The Lord is with me
, of this I am sure
For every day He helps me,
my trials to endure

Psalm 100:1
For the Lord is good; his mercy
is everlasting; and his trith
endureth to all.

THE LORD IS OUR KEEPER

The Lord is our keeper, the Lord is our guide
The Lord will always be on our side
We are His people sought out,
called and chosen of the Lord
And He will do what we ask if we believe
And keep His word in our heart

The devil is trying to destroy God's people
But we won't let this happen because
Jesus Christ, the Lord is our keeper
Let us hold fast to His unchanging hand
And he will lead us into His promised land.

We'll be able to look at the devil and laugh in his face
Because he cannot enter into God's holy place
So let's keep on and obey the Lord
For truly we shall receive our just reward.

THE SOUND OF A WAVE

The sound of a wave is like the sweet sound
Of water splashing against a shallow rock.
Sometimes it can make your mind race forward
Like the ticking of a clock
going tick, tock, tick, tock
The sound of a wave is pleasant
And it can be felt within the heart.
It makes you feel like holding onto memories
Of good times and letting the sad times
From your heart depart
The sound of a wave is very peaceful
And gives you a calmness within your soul
Just listen to the sound of a wave
And you'll have a beautiful moment to behold

*The peace of God is like a compass
for our souls, leading us in the direction
the Holy Spirit intends for our lives.*

THERE IS A JESUS

When I was small and I didn't think I was tall
Because I was very little
and didn't have any height at all
I'm speaking of the natural part of my life
Where there was a lot of envy, jealousy and strife
There is a spiritual side there now
I turned to Jesus and He taught me
He taught me how to love.
He gave me peace
He granted to me grace to stay in this race
Now I'm tall and don't ever have to feel small
Because I gave my life to Jesus,
He is my all in all
I am speaking of my spiritual life now you see
Because there is a Jesus
and He lives in me
There is a Jesus, a Jesus you see
There is a Jesus and He lives in me

THIS TOO SHALL PASS

I passed your house the other day.
As I walked pass your window pane,
I saw tears as if they were great drops of rain.
You were so torn up, you were very depressed.
I said "Lord, please help this soul to find your rest."

When darkness comes to overshadow you.
The devil wants you not to know what to do,
so don't let him get the best of you.
For God has brought you thus far
and he will carry you through.

So dry up your tears and don't be ashamed.
You don't have to cry great tears as if of rain.
So dry up your tears and don't be sorrowful
for God is here today and He will be here tomorrow.

I passed by your house today
and as I passed by your window pane,
I saw a great smile , a smile as of heavenly gain.

TIRED

Are you tired of the world and all it's silly games?
Are you tired of big old sickening jokes
and all of this world's fame?
Are you tired of being down
and answering to the devil all the time?
Aren't you tired of not being able to tell the devil to let go,
And not getting beaten up by him anymore?

You hear people saying "I am tired of this
and I am tired of that".
But do you ever hear people say,
"I wanna go where Jesus is at".
Stop playing around don't be tired and always down.
Turn to Jesus and He'll let you stomp the devil's ground.

If you are tired, discouraged and blue.
Turn to Jesus, He'll tell you what to do.
He'll open doors for you that no natural man can see.
He'll pave the road for you if it's His will that you'll let be.

So come on now, and stop playing around.
Take on Jesus' name and your life won't be the same.
For He is so good, so precious and true
And you won't get tired of Him telling you what to do.

TO ALL MOTHERS

To the mothers who are under the sound of my voice
Please listen as I speak from a sincere heart.
The Lord has dealt with me, you see
That we as mothers are very dear.
He gave us a job to do down here
To take care of his little ones
for they are very dear
They are special, just as we are,
in the sight of the Lord.
The Lord made us mothers
and put His love in our hearts.
Sometimes it seems we don't know
which way to turn
Jesus keeps on helping us
and making us strong.
He is our Savior, holy and true
So mothers let's be strong in the Lord
and do what He wants us to do.

TRUST HIM

When you are alone and feeling in distress,
Look up to Jesus and He'll give you rest
Trust Him !
And don't be discouraged
and don't be dismayed
You know when Jesus came back
To this world He stayed
Trust Him !
You don't have to walk around
with your head hanging down
You don't have to wear on your face
an old wrinkled frown
Trust Him!
Hold your head up
and walk in faith
Jesus will be right there
and He'll lead you straight
Trust Him!

TRUTHS

We shall not slumber
and we shall not sleep
For our lives in His holy hands
He has promised to keep
Look down to none look up to only one
Jesus, for to Mary, the virgin, He was born
Our cross is not too hard to bare
For His, he bore, while in His heart
Was our heavenly kingdom fare.
Jesus is so merciful
His mercy He shares
For to keep our souls
in His own showering care.
The saints are not ignorant,
it's common to see
For in the church of Jesus Christ
is the Holy mercy seat.
We cannot go down the ladder of prayer
For by prayer we will receive
our heavenly kingdom's fare.

TRY HIM AND SEE

The Lord helps me, I knew He would
Does things that you and I never could
He's always there are ready to share
I find it not hard to bear
When I'm in trouble
He's always there
He lets me know that He does care
I am very true, sincere and thankful
For the Lord who has done so much for me
Opens doors for me to see
He hears my plea and answers me
The Lord knows that I am me
He's always there in that time of need
He loves me and He takes heed
He never fails or forsakes me
Why don't you try Him today and see

WALK ON SAINTS

As you travel on your journey
doing the best that you can
Don't drop your hand in despair
when it seems that others don't understand
Walk on in the hope of the Lord
And let Him continue to hold your hand
When the devil tries to make you stray
Jesus will be there to carry you the rest of the way
Hold on saints, hold on!
For Jesus is near to keep
and make you strong
You see, Jesus is listening
to your every call
He'll hold you up if you wish not to fall
So be encouraged in the Lord
Love Him with a sincere heart
Walk in His light and
He will bring you out all right

WALKING DOWN LIFE'S WAY

While walking down life's way,
don't let the devil step in your way.
Don't let him give you an inch
He'll try and make you take a mile.
He'll even try and hold your hand
So that in God's love you can't abide .
While walking down life's way,
Don't let the devil step in your way.
He'll let everything magnify itself
So that you won't to be able to pray
He wants to get you in a jumble
So that your life will be a great big stumble.
He wants you to stumble
He wants you to fall
He just wants you to lose
your eternal life, that's all.
So while walking down life's way
Don't let the devil step in your way.
In Jesus name we can conquer all.

WHAT GOD HAS DONE FOR ME

Jesus has done so much for me;
things the carnal eye can't see
He has given me perfect peace.
He has lifted burdens off me
He has put joy in my soul, new shoes on my feet
He has given me perfect peace;
peace that the devil can't defeat
I am determined to run this race to the end
and I don't have a doubt
That when I reach heaven's gates,
Jesus is gonna let me in.
He has given me peace of mind
He has bestowed love upon me
that can't be defined
He has cleansed my heart
and in it let the sun shine
Jesus has done so much for me, I say
Things that the carnal eye can't see
While running this race to reap and reach my goal
I will not let my testimony go untold
I am determined to make it through
I am determined, my friend, what about you?
Jesus has done so much for me;
things the carnal eye can't see

WHAT GOD HAS GIVEN ME

What God has given me, can't no man take away
God has given me love, can't no man take it away
God has given me understanding, I will not go astray
I will be tempted, I will be tried,
but in Jesus' temple I will continue to abide.
Some might look and some might wonder
I know in Jesus name I will not stumble.
What God has given me, can't no man take away.
God gave me the morningHe gave me the light
He gave me his guiding angel to guide me right
What God has given me, can't no man take away
He gave me ears to hearHe gave me eyes to see
What God has done for me he can do for you too. Hear!
What God has given me, can't no man take away.
God has put me in His holy garden
so that by the devil I won't be trodden.
He has done so many things for me
Things that the carnal eye just can't see
What God has given me, can't no man take away
God has me folded in His loving arms to stay
What God has given me, can't no man take away

WHAT IT MEANS TO ME

God gave me eyes that I can see
He placed His Holy Ghost love in my heart
He gave me a brand new start
This is what it means to me
Jesus lifted me up when I was down
Jesus placed my feet on solid ground
He gave me understanding in my heart
Sweet Jesus gave me a brand new start
This is what it means to me
Once I was walking in the world of sin
I didn't know my enemies from my friends
Jesus sent his angels and led me on in
This is what it means to me
My soul was bound with selfish pride
The devil had me wrapped up and walking in stride
I needed someone to break the yoke
To help me out without a doubt.
Jesus came along and saved my soul
Now I don't have to be ruled by the devil anymore
I can jump and shout and praise his name
For thanks to the Holy Ghost my whole life has changed
This is what it means to me

WHAT JESUS HAS DONE

Jesus made the sunshine , He made the dew
Jesus cleared the path to heaven for you to walk through
He caused the lightning to flash.
He caused the thunder to roar
He caused the rain to fall upon
pon the tender plants for to grow

Jesus made the lame to walk
and calmed the raging sea
Jesus made the dumb to talk
and He healed the leprosy
Knowing Jesus did all of these things
There's no question of what Jesus has in store for you

Jesus made the blind to see
He died on the cross to set us free
He never said not one word
as they nailed Him to the cross
He hung there and did His father's will
so that our souls would not be lost

Jesus loves you, I can say,
in this garden He wants you to be
There's rest here that the carnal eye can't see
He put it here for His souls
who have been set free
Hold your head up and rejoice in Jesus
for with Him you will always win

Don't take for spite the things that are right,
Just serve the Lord with all of your might
Remember to always do Jesus' will
and in His grace you'll continue to live

Love the lord with your whole heart
and from His grace you'll never depart
Always do the best that you can
and in Jesus name take your stand
Jesus will continue to hold your hand
Just keep standing, stand and stand

WHAT MORE CAN I DO?

What more can I do?
What more can I do
to please my Father in heaven?
What more can I do?
For I know he cares for me
He strengthens my soul
and He comforts my heart
He gives me power over evil
When I'm feeling alone, He comes to me
And says,"My Child, don't worry
For I'm right here with you.
I'll never forsake you my child.
I'll never leave you alone.
What more can I do?
What more can I do
to please my Father in heaven?

WHEN IT SEEMS YOU CAN'T GO ON

When it seems like you can't go on
Turn to the man who can make you strong
Jesus is His name, it always will be
He's the one who can set your soul free.

When you seem disappointed with grief
Turn to the man who can set your soul free.
Jesus is His name , its His name can't you see.
He does wonderful things
for the man who wants to be set free.

When the world seems full of trouble and strife,
Turn to Jesus, He will take over and control your life.
Yield all you have to the Father above
And let Him hold you tenderly in His love.
Fret not your heart of evil doers
For Jesus is able to conquer the cruel.

Turn your eyes away from trouble and strife ,
Do not walk in contempt or pride.
Look up to Jesus
In His outstretched hands you can abide.

Hold on to Jesus He'll help you to stand
He won't let go of your wandering hand.
He knows your heart,
He'll answer each prayer.
He knows your troubles
and He heeds to your cares

So when it seems that you can't go on
Look up toward heaven
at God's holy throne.
Imagine Him sitting there just to hear your plea
And with gladness of heart,
He will come see about thee.

Psalm 121:1-2
I will lift up mine eyes unto the hills, from
whence cometh my help. My help cometh from
the Lord which made heacen and earth.

WHEN LIFE GETS HARD

When you have a problem
and you don't know what to do
Talk to Jesus, He'll help you through.
He's the one who sits beside His father's throne
He'll hold your hand ever so dearly in His own.

When you are in a trial and times get hard.
Turn it over to Jesus
For He called you from the very start.
Don't be downcast and don't be dismayed
For Jesus has called you
for your soul to be saved.

When you are on the battlefield
and it seem you are all alone
Call out to Jesus, I know He'll make you strong.
Don't give over to the devil
For he had no power
For it is Jesus who keeps your soul hour after hour.

WHO NEEDS WHO?

We need each other but we need God most.
Who has the right to boast
of who they do and don't need
when it comes to the Holy Ghost?
We have to pattern our lives in the way
that Jesus would have us to go.
For in the awful world of sin
He don't want us to go no more.
We need each other but we need God most
We'll just keep on holding on and we won't let go
We'll walk with an upight heart and a holy mind
For a truth, Jesus will be with us all the time.
Times will come when it seems like we can't go on
But Jesus will continue to hold our hands
and help us to be strong.
Jesus brought us this way
because our lives he wished to save
We will run on, we will run on
and in grace we will win this Jesus name race.
We need each other but we need God most
We won't go down for we have Jesus on our side.
He'll fight our battles for in Him we abide.
We will not be held back by silly thoughts or foolish pride.
We need each other but we need God most
We'll keep right on walking in the Holy Ghost

WITH JOY

With joy I can hold my hands up toward the sky
With joy I can run and not get tired
With joy I can praise God up above
With joy I can keep away envy and strife
With joy I can run this race to the end
With joy I can mount up for my flight
And the devil can't take me in his plight
With joy I can conquer the evil doers
And not be overthrown by the quick pursuers
With joy I am ready to live for God
And take on anything that' comes too hard
I am ready to run and not get weary
Praise God in happiness and not in tears
With God I can take on anything that comes
And not let the devil make me look dumb
With joy Paul preached the word of God
Neither did he let the enemy make things seem hard
With joy he preached the gospel to the end
Nor was it found in his preaching any line that was thin
His preaching was full of Jesus name words
And he turned that old devil around in twirls
With joy he ate the good of the land
With joy he served God until the end
With joy I will go on and Praise my God
And let the devil have the world as his maker to regard.

WITHOUT JESUS

Without Jesus I would be lost
Without Jesus I couldn't go on
I owe it all to Jesus
He who sits on the throne
It's He who teaches us right from wrong
He's ever near; His love is so dear
When I was deceived I felt that I would never be relieved
Jesus sent His angel then I began to believe
I realize that God controls all
And without Jesus my soul would be lost
He holds the world in His hands
And He lets me know that He understands
Sometimes old Satan makes us feel
As if we can't go on
Then Jesus sends one to keep us strong
He is always there
He lets us know that His people care
Without Jesus I would be lost
Jesus is real His love I feel
His life I am learning to live
He sent His angel to help me in His grace
to keep still for without Jesus I would be lost

YOUR MOTHER

God gave her to you
Love her
She can help you and she can care for you
Love her
When she makes an error, try to look past it
Love her
Try not to treat your mother wrong
Love her
Maybe you don't understand
that she"s in God's hands
Love her
Even when your mother is gone
God will strengthen and make you strong
Love her
God holds her in his care
And in His care He holds you there
Love her

About The Author

Ms. Lena F. Cole lives in Houston, Tx. She was born and reared in Monroe and Calhoun, Louisiana. Her fondest desire has always been to be able to sow into the lives of others. To this end, she entered the teaching profession and taught in the Spring Independent School District for several years.

Writing has always been her joy and she began writing at an early age. Lena is a born-again Christian who loves to share her spiritual beliefs and insight in her poems and stories. Her faith has been made strong in adversity. Every day has not been perfect but she constantly shares her faith in a perfect God. Gaining and sharing her wisdom is a huge motivator in her life.

She is the mother of two children and two grandchildren. Her life demonstrates that with prayer and perseverance anything is possible.

www.ingramcontent.com/pod-product-compliance
Lightning Source LLC
LaVergne TN
LVHW021403080426
835508LV00020B/2437